The Ultimate Guide to Print-on-Demand T-Shirts: Launching a Successful Apparel Business

I0505041

Welcome to "The Ultimate Guide to Print-on-Demand T-Shirts: Launching a Successful Apparel Business." In this comprehensive ebook, we will delve into the exciting world of print-on-demand (POD) t-shirts, equipping you with the knowledge and strategies to create and thrive in a profitable print-on-demand apparel venture. Whether you're a creative entrepreneur, a fashion enthusiast, or someone looking to explore a new business opportunity, this guide will take you through every step of the process.

Table of Contents:

Understanding Print-on-Demand T-Shirts

1.1 What is Print-on-Demand?

Print on Demand (POD) is a modern publishing and manufacturing model that allows for the production of physical products on an as-needed basis. It is a digital printing process that eliminates the need for large print runs and extensive inventory storage. Instead, products are created individually or in small quantities in direct response to customer orders.

The core principle of Print on Demand is the digitization of content and designs. Books, apparel, merchandise, and other products are stored and managed in digital formats, reducing the reliance on physical inventory. When an order is received, the product is printed or manufactured, often using digital printing technologies, and then promptly shipped to the customer.

Print on Demand offers several benefits and advantages. First, it significantly reduces upfront production costs and eliminates the risk of unsold inventory. This accessibility makes it feasible for independent authors, small businesses, and creative individuals to enter the market without substantial financial investment. Additionally, it allows for flexibility and scalability, as products can be easily adjusted in response to changing demand.

One of the key advantages of Print on Demand is its efficiency in distribution. Many Print on Demand platforms integrate with online marketplaces and fulfillment centers, streamlining the order fulfillment process and enabling easy distribution to customers worldwide. This eliminates the need for individual businesses to manage complex logistics or establish their own distribution networks.

Furthermore, Print on Demand is considered a sustainable approach to manufacturing. By producing items only when there is a confirmed order, it minimizes waste and reduces environmental impact. This aligns with the growing demand for eco-friendly practices and ethical consumption.

Print on Demand has disrupted various industries. In the publishing sector, it has revolutionized self-publishing, allowing authors to bring their books to market without relying on traditional publishing houses. In the apparel and merchandise industry, it has enabled brands to offer customizable products and limited editions without the burden of inventory management. It has also found applications in education, art, and other creative fields.

Overall, Print on Demand has transformed the way products are created, published, and distributed. With its cost-effectiveness, scalability, and sustainability, it has empowered individuals and businesses to bring their ideas and creations to a global audience, making it a popular choice in the modern marketplace.

1.2 Why Choose Print-on-Demand for T-Shirts?

Choosing print on demand (POD) offers several compelling reasons and advantages for individuals and businesses. Here are some key factors to consider:

Cost-Effectiveness: Print on demand eliminates the need for large upfront investments in inventory. Traditional publishing and manufacturing models often require significant financial resources to produce and store inventory, leading to the risk of unsold products. With POD, you only pay for items as they are ordered, minimizing financial risks and allowing for a more efficient allocation of resources.

Reduced Overhead and Logistics: POD eliminates the need for inventory storage and management. Without the burden of warehousing, fulfillment, and shipping, you can focus more on product development, marketing, and growing your business. POD platforms often handle the entire fulfillment process, including printing, packaging, and shipping, saving you time and effort.

Flexibility and Scalability: Print on demand offers flexibility in product customization and scalability in response to demand. You can easily update designs, experiment with new products, and tailor offerings to specific customer preferences without the constraints of minimum order quantities or excessive production lead times. This agility allows you to adapt quickly to market trends and customer feedback.

Global Reach and Accessibility: POD platforms typically integrate with online marketplaces, providing access to a vast customer base worldwide. You can reach customers in different countries without the complexities of international shipping and logistics. This global reach expands your potential audience and increases the chances of your products being discovered and purchased by customers around the world.

Reduced Waste and Sustainability: Traditional manufacturing often leads to overproduction and excess inventory, resulting in waste. Print on demand minimizes waste by producing items only when there is a confirmed order. This sustainable approach aligns with environmental consciousness and reduces the negative impact on the planet.

Lower Barrier to Entry: POD eliminates many traditional barriers to entry in industries like publishing and fashion. Aspiring authors, artists, and entrepreneurs can enter the market with minimal upfront costs, making it more accessible to individuals who may not have the resources to invest in large-scale production. This democratization of opportunities allows for greater creativity, diversity, and innovation in the marketplace.

Quick Time-to-Market: With print on demand, you can bring products to market swiftly. There are no lengthy production cycles or waiting for large print runs to be completed. As soon as your designs are finalized and uploaded to the platform, they can be available for purchase, allowing you to capitalize on trends, seasonal demand, or time-sensitive opportunities.

1.3 The Advantages of Print-on-Demand Apparel

The advantages of print-on-demand apparel include cost-effectiveness, flexibility, reduced risk, faster time-to-market, global reach, scalability, minimal infrastructure requirements, and a reduced environmental impact. These advantages make print-on-demand an appealing option for entrepreneurs, independent designers, and businesses looking to enter or expand in the apparel market. Print-on-Demand (POD) apparel offers several advantages that make it an attractive option for individuals and businesses. Here are some key advantages of print-on-demand apparel:

Cost-Effective: Traditional apparel manufacturing often requires large upfront investments in inventory, production, and storage. With print-on-demand apparel, you eliminate the need for pre-producing and storing inventory. Products are manufactured on-demand as orders are received, reducing the financial risk associated with unsold stock. This cost-effective approach allows for more efficient resource allocation and reduces the need for significant capital investment upfront.

Flexibility and Customization: Print-on-demand apparel provides the flexibility to offer a wide range of designs, styles, and variations without the need for minimum order quantities. This flexibility enables you to cater to diverse customer preferences and target specific niches or market segments. You can easily experiment with different designs, color options, and sizes to meet the demands of your customers.

Reduced Risk and Inventory Management: With print-on-demand apparel, you don't have to worry about forecasting demand accurately or managing inventory levels. Since products are produced as orders come in, you can avoid the risk of overstocking or understocking. This reduces the costs associated with excess inventory, warehousing, and potential losses from outdated or unsold items.

Faster Time-to-Market: Traditional apparel manufacturing involves longer lead times for production, shipping, and distribution. Print-on-demand apparel significantly reduces these lead times, allowing you to bring products to market quickly. Once a design is finalized, it can be made available for sale immediately, enabling you to capitalize on trends, seasonal demand, or time-sensitive opportunities.

Global Reach and Scalability: Print-on-demand platforms often have integrated fulfillment and shipping capabilities, which enable seamless distribution to customers worldwide. You can reach a global audience without the complexities of international shipping and logistics. As your business grows, the scalability of print-on-demand allows for easy expansion, as production can be scaled up or down based on demand.

Minimal Overhead and Infrastructure: Setting up a print-on-demand apparel business requires minimal infrastructure compared to traditional manufacturing. You don't need to invest in specialized equipment or maintain a dedicated production facility. The print-on-demand platform handles the printing, packaging, and shipping processes, allowing you to focus on product design, marketing, and customer engagement.

Reduced Environmental Impact: Print-on-demand apparel is often considered a more sustainable approach to manufacturing. Since products are made on-demand, there is less waste from overproduction or excess inventory. Additionally, digital printing technologies used in print-on-demand often have lower water and energy consumption compared to traditional printing methods, reducing the environmental footprint.

1.4 Exploring Design Options and Techniques

Exploring Design Options and Techniques for Print on Demand (POD) allows you to create unique and appealing products that stand out in the marketplace. Here are some key considerations and techniques to enhance your design options for POD:

Graphic Design: Invest time and effort into creating visually compelling and engaging designs. Consider factors such as color schemes, typography, composition, and visual hierarchy. Experiment with different design styles, whether it's minimalistic, illustrative, vintage, or modern, to cater to diverse customer preferences.

Product-Specific Design: Tailor your designs to the specific products you are offering. Keep in mind the shape, size, and printable area of the product. Adapt your design elements to complement the product's dimensions, ensuring that they appear cohesive and visually appealing when printed on the final product.

Customization and Personalization: Take advantage of the customization options offered by print-on-demand platforms. Allow customers to personalize their chosen products by adding names, initials, or custom text. This enhances the customer experience and makes the product more unique and meaningful to them.

Trend Analysis: Stay updated with current design trends and incorporate them into your work. Research popular themes, color palettes, and styles that resonate with your target audience. However, balance following trends with maintaining your unique creative voice to avoid being too derivative.

Seasonal and Event-Based Designs: Consider creating designs that align with specific seasons, holidays, or events. This can include themed designs for Christmas, Halloween, Valentine's Day, or designs for special occasions like birthdays or weddings. Capitalize on these opportunities to attract customers looking for relevant and timely products.

Mockups and Product Visualization: Utilize mockup templates provided by print-on-demand platforms or create your own. These templates allow you to showcase your designs on product mockups, providing customers with a visual representation of how the final product will look. High-quality product visualization helps customers make informed purchasing decisions.

Layering and Textures: Experiment with layering different design elements and incorporating textures to add depth and visual interest. This technique can enhance the overall aesthetic appeal of your designs, making them more engaging and visually captivating.

Vector Graphics and High-Resolution Images: Use vector graphics or high-resolution images in your designs to ensure optimal print quality. These formats allow for scalability without loss of quality, ensuring that your designs appear crisp and professional on various product sizes.

Branding and Packaging: Develop a cohesive brand identity and ensure that your design elements align with your brand. Consistent branding across your product line builds recognition and trust with customers. Additionally, consider designing custom packaging or branding inserts that enhance the overall presentation and perceived value of your products.

Customer Feedback and Iteration: Actively seek and consider customer feedback on your designs. Pay attention to what designs resonate with your audience and make adjustments based on their preferences. Iteration based on customer input helps refine your designs and leads to better customer satisfaction.

By exploring various design options and techniques for print on demand, you can create visually appealing and marketable products that cater to your target audience's preferences. Regularly experimenting, iterating, and staying updated with design trends will help you stay competitive and continually evolve your product offerings.

Setting Up Your Print-on-Demand T-Shirt Business

2.1 Defining Your Target Audience and Niche

Defining your target audience and niche is a crucial step in maximizing the success of your print-on-demand (POD) business. It involves identifying the specific group of people who are most likely to be interested in your products and tailoring your designs and marketing efforts to cater to their needs and preferences. Here's a breakdown of the process:

Market Research: Conduct thorough market research to gain insights into the existing demand and competition in the POD industry. Identify the broader market trends, customer segments, and popular product categories within the POD space. Analyze successful POD businesses and study their target audience to understand their strategies and positioning.

Demographics and Psychographics: Define the demographics of your target audience, including factors such as age, gender, location, occupation, and income level. Additionally, consider the psychographic characteristics, such as interests, hobbies, lifestyles, and values. Understanding these aspects helps you create designs and marketing messages that resonate with your audience.

Niche Identification: Narrow down your target audience by identifying a specific niche or subcategory within the larger POD market. This allows you to focus your efforts and differentiate yourself from competitors. Your niche could be based on specific interests, passions, hobbies, or even profession-related themes. By catering to a niche, you can develop a more targeted and loyal customer base.

Customer Personas: Create customer personas or profiles that represent your ideal target audience segments. These personas are fictional characters that embody the characteristics and preferences of your potential customers. Include details such as demographics, interests, motivations, and shopping behaviors. This exercise helps you better understand and empathize with your customers, guiding your design and marketing decisions.

Competitor Analysis: Study your competitors who are targeting a similar audience or operating within the same niche. Analyze their product offerings, design styles, pricing strategies, and marketing approaches. Identify gaps or areas where you can differentiate yourself and offer unique value to your target audience.

Value Proposition: Develop a clear value proposition that outlines the unique benefits and advantages your products offer to your target audience. This could include factors like superior design quality, customization options, affordable pricing, or fast shipping. Highlighting your unique selling points helps attract and retain customers within your target market.

Feedback and Iteration: Actively seek feedback from your target audience as you develop and launch your products. Engage with your customers through social media, surveys, or product reviews to understand their preferences, pain points, and suggestions. Incorporate their feedback into your future designs and product offerings to continually refine and improve your offerings.

Remember, defining your target audience and niche is an ongoing process. It requires continuous monitoring of market trends, customer feedback, and evolving customer preferences. By understanding and catering to your target audience, you can develop products and marketing strategies that resonate with them, leading to increased customer engagement and loyalty.

2.2 Choosing the Right Print-on-Demand Platform

Choosing the right print-on-demand (POD) platform is crucial for the success of your business. Here are some key factors to consider when evaluating and selecting a POD platform:

Product Variety and Quality: Assess the range of products offered by the platform. Look for a diverse selection of apparel, accessories, home decor, and other customizable items that align with your target audience's preferences. Additionally, consider the quality of the products, including the fabric, printing techniques, and overall craftsmanship. High-quality products contribute to customer satisfaction and repeat purchases.

Printing Technology and Capabilities: Evaluate the printing technology used by the platform. Look for options like direct-to-garment (DTG) printing or dye sublimation that provide vibrant and durable prints. Consider the platform's ability to handle complex designs, intricate details, and color accuracy. The printing capabilities of the platform directly impact the final product quality and customer satisfaction.

Customization Options: Assess the level of customization available on the platform. Look for features like design templates, text editing tools, and image manipulation capabilities. The platform should allow you to easily customize and personalize your products to meet the specific needs and preferences of your target audience. The more flexible the customization options, the better you can cater to customer demands.

User-Friendly Interface: Consider the user experience and ease of use of the platform's interface. A user-friendly interface makes it easier for you to create and manage your products, upload designs, set pricing, and track sales and orders. Look for platforms with intuitive navigation, clear instructions, and responsive customer support to ensure a smooth and efficient workflow.

Integration with E-commerce Channels: If you plan to sell your products through your own website or online marketplaces, check if the platform offers seamless integration with popular e-commerce channels. Look for integrations with platforms like Shopify, WooCommerce, Etsy, or Amazon, as they can simplify your sales process and expand your reach to a wider customer base.

Pricing Structure and Profit Margins: Evaluate the pricing structure of the platform, including product costs, printing fees, and shipping rates. Compare these costs to your desired profit margins to ensure that selling through the platform aligns with your business goals. Consider any membership or subscription fees associated with using the platform and factor them into your pricing strategy.

Fulfillment and Shipping Services: Consider the platform's fulfillment and shipping services. Look for options like automated order processing, tracking capabilities, and reliable shipping partners. Efficient and timely order fulfillment contributes to customer satisfaction, and transparent tracking systems allow you and your customers to monitor the progress of orders.

Customer Support: Assess the level of customer support provided by the platform. Look for platforms that offer responsive and helpful customer support channels, such as email, live chat, or phone support. Prompt and reliable customer support is crucial when you have questions, encounter issues, or need assistance with your orders or account.

Reputation and Reviews: Research the platform's reputation and read reviews from other users. Look for feedback on the platform's reliability, print quality, customer service, and overall user experience. User reviews can provide valuable insights into the platform's strengths and weaknesses, helping you make an informed decision.

Terms and Ownership: Review the platform's terms and conditions, especially regarding ownership of your designs and intellectual property rights. Ensure that you retain ownership of your designs and have the freedom to use them on other platforms or for other purposes.

By carefully considering these factors, you can choose a POD platform that aligns with your business goals, offers the right product selection and customization options, provides reliable printing and fulfillment services, and supports your overall success in the print-on-demand industry.

2.3 Copyright Considerations for T-Shirt Designs

Copyright considerations are crucial when it comes to creating and selling t-shirt designs. Here are some key points to keep in mind:

Originality: Ensure that your t-shirt designs are original and not copied or heavily influenced by existing copyrighted works. Copyright law protects original creative works, including visual art, illustrations, and designs. Creating your own unique designs will help you avoid infringing on someone else's copyright.

Public Domain: Some works fall into the public domain, meaning they are no longer protected by copyright and can be freely used. However, determining the public domain status of a work can be complex, as it varies based on factors such as the creator's lifespan and the specific laws of your jurisdiction. It is advisable to conduct thorough research or seek legal advice if you plan to use public domain works.

Fair Use: Fair use allows limited use of copyrighted works for specific purposes, such as commentary, criticism, or parody. However, the application of fair use can be subjective and depends on factors such as the nature of the copyrighted work, the purpose of your t-shirt design, and the extent of the use. If you believe your design falls under fair use, it is recommended to consult with a legal professional for guidance.

Permission and Licensing: If you want to use copyrighted material in your t-shirt designs, such as quotes, logos, or artwork created by others, it is essential to obtain proper permission or licensing. Contact the copyright holder or seek out licenses available through stock image websites or design marketplaces. Ensure that the permissions or licenses obtained are clear, specific to your intended use, and legally valid.

Parody and Satire: Parody and satire can be protected under copyright law as a form of free expression. However, it is important to understand the distinction between a legitimate parody and a design that simply copies or appropriates existing copyrighted works. Parody should involve transformative elements and comment on or critique the original work in a noticeable and substantial way.

Trademark Considerations: In addition to copyright, be aware of trademark issues. Trademarks protect brand names, logos, and symbols that identify specific companies or products. Avoid using trademarks in your designs without proper authorization, as it can lead to legal disputes. Research and ensure that your designs do not infringe on any existing trademarks.

Design Ownership: As a creator, you should understand the ownership rights of your own designs. If you work for a company or as a freelancer, there may be contractual agreements that determine who owns the rights to the designs you create. Clarify ownership and usage rights before selling or licensing your designs for t-shirts.

2.4 Establishing a Strong Brand Identity

Establishing a strong brand identity is essential for differentiating your print-on-demand (POD) business and building a loyal customer base. It involves creating a unique and consistent brand image that resonates with your target audience. Here are some key steps to help you establish a strong brand identity:

Define Your Brand's Personality: Start by defining the personality and values that your brand represents. Consider the emotions and associations you want customers to have when they interact with your brand. Are you aiming for a fun and playful image, or do you prefer a more sophisticated and professional vibe? Clearly articulate your brand's personality to guide your design and marketing decisions.

Develop a Brand Name and Logo: Create a memorable brand name that reflects your business and resonates with your target audience. Design a logo that visually represents your brand's personality and communicates its essence. Ensure that your logo is versatile and works well across various mediums and platforms.

Design Consistent Visual Elements: Establish a consistent visual identity by selecting a color palette, typography, and other design elements that align with your brand's personality. Use these elements consistently across your website, product packaging, social media profiles, and marketing materials. Consistency in visual elements helps customers recognize and remember your brand.

Craft a Compelling Brand Story: Develop a brand story that communicates your business's purpose, values, and unique selling proposition. Your brand story should be authentic, engaging, and resonate with your target audience. Use your brand story to create an emotional connection with customers, allowing them to relate to your brand on a deeper level.

Define Brand Voice and Messaging: Determine the tone of voice that your brand will use in its communications. Whether it's friendly, authoritative, conversational, or humorous, your brand voice should align with your target audience's preferences. Develop key messaging points that highlight your brand's value proposition and differentiate you from competitors.

Consistent Customer Experience: Ensure that your brand identity is reflected in every customer touchpoint. From website design and product packaging to customer service interactions, strive for a consistent and positive customer experience. Consistency in your brand's look, feel, and messaging across different touchpoints reinforces your brand identity and builds trust.

Engage on Social Media: Leverage social media platforms to actively engage with your audience and build brand awareness. Share visually appealing content, showcase your products, and participate in conversations relevant to your niche. Develop a social media strategy that aligns with your brand's personality and encourages community engagement.

Seek Brand Partnerships and Collaborations: Consider partnering with influencers, bloggers, or other brands that align with your target audience and brand values. Collaborative efforts can help you reach new audiences and strengthen your brand's credibility. Choose partnerships that complement your brand and contribute to its overall image.

Deliver Quality and Consistency: Maintain a high level of quality in your products, designs, and customer service. Consistently deliver on your brand promises to build trust and loyalty among your customers. Positive experiences and quality products contribute to word-of-mouth referrals and repeat business.

Evolve and Adapt: As your business grows and the market evolves, be open to refining and adapting your brand identity. Regularly assess customer feedback, market trends, and competitor strategies to ensure that your brand remains relevant and resonates with your target audience.

By following these steps, you can establish a strong brand identity for your print-on-demand business. A cohesive and authentic brand identity helps you stand out in the marketplace, build customer loyalty, and create a lasting impression with your target audience.

Designing Your Print-on-Demand T-Shirts

3.1 Identifying Popular T-Shirt Design Styles

Identifying popular t-shirt design styles is essential for creating appealing and marketable designs that resonate with your target audience. Here are some popular t-shirt design styles to consider:

Minimalist: Minimalist designs focus on simplicity and clean aesthetics. They often feature minimal elements, simple shapes, and limited color palettes. Minimalist designs can convey a sense of sophistication and modernity.

Typography: Typography-based designs use creative and expressive typography as the main visual element. This style emphasizes the arrangement, size, and style of the text to convey the message or create a visual impact. Typography designs can be playful, bold, or elegant, depending on the chosen fonts and layout.

Vintage and Retro: Vintage and retro designs draw inspiration from past eras, such as the 60s, 70s, or 80s. They feature distressed textures, faded colors, and nostalgic imagery. Vintage designs can evoke a sense of nostalgia and appeal to those who appreciate a retro aesthetic.

Illustrative: Illustrative designs incorporate detailed and artistic illustrations as the main focal point. They can range from intricate line drawings to vibrant and colorful graphics. Illustrative designs allow for creativity and storytelling, making them popular among various audiences.

Pop Culture and Fandom: Designs inspired by popular culture, movies, TV shows, or iconic characters have a wide appeal among fans. These designs often feature recognizable symbols, quotes, or imagery associated with specific fandoms or cultural references.

Abstract and Geometric: Abstract and geometric designs utilize geometric shapes, patterns, and abstract forms to create visually striking visuals. They often play with symmetry, repetition, and vibrant colors to produce eye-catching designs.

Humor and Sarcasm: Humorous and sarcastic designs use clever wordplay, witty phrases, or funny illustrations to elicit laughter or evoke a sense of irony. These designs cater to individuals who enjoy a lighthearted and humorous approach.

Inspirational and Motivational: Inspirational designs feature uplifting quotes, empowering messages, or motivational imagery. They aim to inspire and encourage positivity, making them popular among individuals seeking motivation or personal growth.

Sports and Athletics: Designs related to sports and athletics resonate with fans and athletes. These designs can feature team logos, sports equipment, or motivational quotes related to sports. They are popular for team spirit, fitness enthusiasts, and sports events.

Nature and Wildlife: Nature-inspired designs incorporate elements like plants, animals, landscapes, or natural elements. They appeal to individuals who appreciate the beauty of the outdoors and have an affinity for nature and wildlife.

It's important to research and stay updated on current design trends and preferences within your target audience. Additionally, consider combining different design styles or adding a unique twist to create designs that stand out and cater to specific niche markets. Experimentation and understanding your audience's preferences will help you identify the most popular t-shirt design styles for your print-on-demand business.

3.2 Creating Compelling and Marketable Designs

Creating compelling and marketable designs is essential for success in the print-on-demand (POD) business. Here are some key tips to help you create designs that capture attention and drive sales:

Know Your Target Audience: Understand the demographics, interests, and preferences of your target audience. Research their design preferences, current trends, and popular themes within your niche. This knowledge will guide your design choices and ensure your designs resonate with your intended customers.

Research Design Trends: Stay updated on the latest design trends relevant to your niche. Explore design blogs, social media platforms, and design marketplaces to gain inspiration and insights into what styles and themes are currently popular. Incorporate elements of these trends while adding your unique twist to stand out.

Focus on Unique and Original Designs: Differentiate yourself by creating unique and original designs that are not readily available elsewhere. Avoid copying or plagiarizing designs, as it can harm your reputation and may have legal implications. Instead, strive for creativity and innovation to offer something fresh and appealing to your target audience.

Balance Visual Appeal and Message: Ensure your designs strike a balance between visual appeal and conveying a clear message. The design should be visually appealing, with attention to composition, color choices, and typography. Simultaneously, consider the intended message, whether it's conveying an emotion, a statement, or aligning with a specific theme or niche.

Use High-Quality Graphics and Assets: Utilize high-quality graphics, illustrations, and assets in your designs. Invest in professional tools, software, or graphic designers if needed, to ensure your designs have a polished and professional look. High-quality visuals contribute to the perceived value of your products.

Consider Placement and Scalability: Keep in mind the placement of your design on the product, such as the front, back, or sleeve of a t-shirt. Ensure the design is scalable and can adapt to different product sizes without losing its impact or readability. Test your designs on various product mockups to ensure they look appealing and coherent in different formats.

Test and Gather Feedback: Before launching a design, consider testing it with a focus group or seeking feedback from your target audience. This feedback can provide valuable insights into the appeal and effectiveness of your design. Iteratively refine and improve your designs based on the feedback received.

Create Design Collections and Themes: Curate design collections or themes that appeal to specific interests or occasions. This allows customers to explore a range of related designs and encourages them to purchase multiple items. Design collections can also create a cohesive brand experience and attract customers who resonate with a particular theme.

Pay Attention to Color Psychology: Colors evoke emotions and can influence customer perception. Understand color psychology and how different colors are associated with specific emotions or meanings. Choose color palettes that align with your design's intended message or theme and resonate with your target audience.

Keep it Simple: Sometimes, simplicity is key. Designs that are clean, minimalistic, and easily understandable can have broad appeal. Focus on conveying your message or capturing attention with clarity rather than overwhelming the design with unnecessary elements.

Remember, creating compelling and marketable designs is an iterative process. Continuously seek feedback, monitor trends, and adapt your designs to meet the evolving preferences of your target audience. With creativity, research, and an understanding of your customers, you can create designs that stand out, connect with your audience, and drive sales in the POD industry.

3.3 Choosing Colors and Fonts

Choosing the right colors and fonts is crucial for creating visually appealing and impactful designs. Here are some considerations when selecting colors and fonts for your print-on-demand designs:

Choosing Colors:

Understand Color Psychology: Different colors evoke different emotions and associations. Consider the psychological impact of colors and choose hues that align with the message or mood you want to convey. For example, warm colors like red and orange can evoke energy and passion, while cool colors like blue and green can create a sense of calmness and harmony.

Consider Brand Identity: If you have an established brand identity, select colors that align with your brand's personality and values. Consistency in color usage across your designs helps strengthen brand recognition and creates a cohesive visual identity.

Contrast and Legibility: Ensure there is enough contrast between your design elements and the background color to maintain legibility and visibility. High contrast helps key elements stand out and ensures that text is readable. Consider color combinations that provide a pleasing contrast while maintaining visual harmony.

Cultural Significance: Be mindful of cultural connotations and symbolism associated with different colors. Colors can hold different meanings and interpretations in various cultures. Research the cultural significance of colors, especially if your target audience is diverse or international.

Use Color Wheel and Palettes: Familiarize yourself with color theory and the color wheel. Experiment with complementary colors (opposite on the color wheel) for vibrant and impactful designs. Explore color palettes and tools available online to find harmonious combinations or create a consistent color scheme for your brand.

Choosing Fonts:

Consider Readability: Prioritize readability when selecting fonts for your designs, especially for any text elements. Choose fonts that are clear, legible, and easy to read at different sizes. Avoid overly decorative or intricate fonts that may hinder readability.

Reflect Brand Personality: Fonts convey a visual tone and personality. Consider the character and style of your brand when selecting fonts. For example, a sleek and modern brand may opt for clean and minimalistic sans-serif fonts, while a vintage-inspired brand may choose serif fonts with ornamental details.

Balance and Hierarchy: Create visual hierarchy by using different font styles, sizes, and weights to emphasize important elements. Use contrasting fonts (e.g., pairing a serif with a sans-serif) to add visual interest and differentiate between headlines, subheadings, and body text.

Consistency and Cohesion: Establish consistency in font usage across your designs and branding materials to maintain a cohesive visual identity. Consistent font choices contribute to brand recognition and help build a sense of familiarity with your audience.

Experiment and Stand Out: While readability and consistency are important, don't be afraid to experiment with unique or custom fonts to add personality and stand out from the competition. Custom fonts can create a distinct and memorable brand identity.

When selecting colors and fonts, it's helpful to create style guides or brand guidelines to ensure consistency in your design choices. These guidelines can serve as a reference for yourself or any designers working on your behalf, ensuring that your colors and fonts align with your brand's identity and resonate with your target audience.

3.4 Utilizing Design Tools and Resources

Utilizing design tools and resources can greatly enhance your print-on-demand (POD) business by streamlining your design process, improving the quality of your designs, and boosting your productivity. Here are some key design tools and resources you can utilize:

Graphic Design Software: Adobe Photoshop, Adobe Illustrator, and CorelDRAW are industry-standard graphic design software programs that provide a wide range of tools and capabilities for creating and editing designs. These programs offer advanced features and allow for precise control over design elements.

Online Design Tools: Online design platforms such as Canva, Crello, and Pixlr provide user-friendly interfaces and pre-made templates that can simplify the design process. These tools offer a wide variety of design elements, fonts, and graphics that you can customize for your print-on-demand products.

Design Marketplaces: Creative marketplaces like Creative Market, Envato Elements, and Design Bundles offer a vast collection of design assets, including fonts, graphics, illustrations, and templates. These resources can save you time and effort in creating designs from scratch and provide inspiration for your own unique creations.

Mockup Generators: Mockup generators like Placeit, Smartmockups, and Yellow Images allow you to easily showcase your designs on various product templates, including t-shirts, hoodies, mugs, and more. These tools provide realistic mockups that help you visualize how your designs will look on actual products.

Font Libraries: Websites like Google Fonts, DaFont, and FontSquirrel offer extensive collections of free and commercial fonts that you can use to enhance your designs. Choose fonts that align with your brand identity and the overall aesthetic you want to achieve.

Color Palette Generators: Color palette generators such as Coolors, Adobe Color, and Paletton help you create harmonious color schemes for your designs. These tools generate complementary and analogous color combinations based on a selected color or theme, allowing you to create visually appealing designs.

Stock Photo Libraries: Stock photo websites like Shutterstock, Unsplash, and Pexels provide a vast array of high-quality images that you can use in your designs. These resources are especially useful when you need professional-quality visuals to complement your designs or create eye-catching compositions.

Online Communities and Forums: Engage with online communities and forums focused on design, such as Behance, Dribbble, and Reddit's r/design subreddit. These platforms offer inspiration, feedback, and the opportunity to connect with other designers and creative professionals.

Design Inspiration Websites: Websites like Awwwards, Dribbble, and Behance showcase exceptional design work from around the world. Explore these platforms to gather inspiration, discover new design trends, and stay updated on the latest industry practices.

Learning Resources: Online learning platforms like Udemy, Skillshare, and YouTube offer a wide range of tutorials and courses on graphic design, typography, color theory, and other design-related topics. Invest time in expanding your design skills and staying up-to-date with the latest techniques and trends.

Remember to use these tools and resources as a starting point and add your unique creative touch to your designs. Experiment, iterate, and continuously refine your design skills to create compelling and marketable designs for your print-on-demand business.

Selecting and Sourcing T-Shirt Blanks

4.1 Understanding T-Shirt Fabrics and Styles

Understanding t-shirt fabrics and styles is essential for selecting the right materials and designs that align with your print-on-demand business. Here are some key points to consider:

T-Shirt Fabrics:

Cotton: Cotton is one of the most common and widely used fabric choices for t-shirts. It is comfortable, breathable, and has good moisture-wicking properties. Cotton t-shirts are versatile and suitable for various occasions.

Polyester: Polyester is a synthetic fabric known for its durability, wrinkle resistance, and quick-drying properties. Polyester t-shirts are often used for athletic or performance wear due to their moisture-wicking abilities. They can also offer vibrant color options.

Blends: T-shirt blends combine different fabric types to leverage the benefits of each material. For example, a cotton-polyester blend can offer the softness of cotton with the durability and moisture-wicking properties of polyester. Blends provide a balance between comfort, performance, and durability.

Triblend: Triblend t-shirts are made from a combination of three materials: cotton, polyester, and rayon. They are known for their softness, lightweight feel, and draping properties. Triblend fabrics often have a vintage or retro aesthetic.

Organic and Sustainable Fabrics: With a growing focus on sustainability, organic cotton and other eco-friendly fabric options have gained popularity. These fabrics are made from organic and pesticide-free materials, minimizing the environmental impact.

T-Shirt Styles:

Crew Neck: Crew neck t-shirts have a round neckline that sits snugly around the base of the neck. They are a classic and versatile choice suitable for casual and everyday wear.

V-Neck: V-neck t-shirts have a neckline that forms a V shape, providing a more open and elongated look. They are popular for a slightly dressier or flattering appearance.

Scoop Neck: Scoop neck t-shirts have a wider and deeper neckline that exposes more of the collarbone and chest area. They offer a more feminine and relaxed style.

Henley: Henley t-shirts feature a buttoned placket or partial button-down front, similar to a polo shirt. They add a touch of detail and can be worn casually or for a more refined look.

Raglan: Raglan t-shirts have sleeves that extend to the collar in one piece, with diagonal seams from the underarm to the neckline. This style is often used in sportswear and lends itself well to contrasting color designs.

Long Sleeve: Long sleeve t-shirts provide extra coverage and warmth, making them suitable for cooler weather or layering. They come in various necklines and can be styled for both casual and more formal occasions.

Tank Tops: Tank tops, also known as sleeveless or muscle shirts, have no sleeves and feature a wider armhole. They are popular for warm weather or as activewear, allowing for maximum arm mobility.

Crop Tops: Crop tops are shorter in length, exposing the midriff or a portion of the abdomen. They offer a trendy and youthful style, often paired with high-waisted bottoms.

Consider your target audience, their preferences, and the intended purpose of the t-shirts when selecting fabrics and styles. It's also important to source high-quality materials that are comfortable, durable, and suitable for printing. Providing a variety of fabric choices and t-shirt styles can cater to different customer preferences and increase the appeal of your print-on-demand products.

4.2 Evaluating Quality and Fit

Evaluating the quality and fit of t-shirts is crucial for ensuring customer satisfaction and maintaining the reputation of your print-on-demand business. Here are some key factors to consider when evaluating the quality and fit of t-shirts:

Fabric Quality: Examine the fabric of the t-shirt to assess its quality. Look for softness, durability, and the overall feel of the material. Consider factors such as thickness, weight, and whether it meets industry standards. High-quality fabrics tend to be comfortable, long-lasting, and resistant to pilling or shrinking.

Stitching and Construction: Inspect the stitching and construction of the t-shirt to determine its quality. Look for well-executed seams that are straight, even, and securely stitched. Double stitching or reinforced stitching on stress points like shoulders and hems can indicate better durability and longevity.

Printability: If you plan to print designs on the t-shirts, consider the printability of the fabric. Some fabrics may be more receptive to different printing techniques, such as screen printing, heat transfer, or direct-to-garment printing. Ensure the fabric has a smooth surface and suitable color saturation for optimal print results.

Fit and Sizing: Evaluate the fit and sizing options available for the t-shirts. Consider factors such as the cut, length, and proportions of the t-shirt. It's important to offer a range of sizes to accommodate various body types and preferences. Take into account both standard sizing and any specific size charts provided by the manufacturer.

Comfort and Mobility: Assess the comfort and mobility offered by the t-shirt. Consider factors such as the ease of movement, breathability, and overall comfort against the skin. A well-fitting and comfortable t-shirt enhances the wearer's experience and increases the likelihood of repeat purchases.

Color Fastness: Check the color fastness of the t-shirt fabric. Colors should be vibrant and resistant to fading or bleeding, especially after multiple washes. Look for t-shirts that have undergone colorfastness testing or are made with high-quality dyes to ensure long-lasting color integrity.

Shrinkage and Stretch: Consider the potential for shrinkage or stretch in the t-shirt fabric. T-shirts that are pre-shrunk or made with fabric blends that minimize shrinkage are preferable. Additionally, fabrics with a degree of stretch or flexibility can provide better comfort and shape retention.

Care Instructions: Review the care instructions provided by the manufacturer. Proper care and maintenance can significantly impact the longevity and appearance of the t-shirt. Clear and accurate care instructions help customers maintain the quality of the product.

Customer Feedback: Pay attention to customer reviews and feedback regarding the quality and fit of the t-shirts. Customer experiences can provide valuable insights into the overall satisfaction with the product, including its quality, durability, and fit.

Supplier Reputation: Evaluate the reputation and credibility of the t-shirt supplier or manufacturer. Research their track record, customer reviews, and any certifications they may have. Working with reputable suppliers ensures consistent quality and reliable sourcing.

By carefully evaluating the quality and fit of t-shirts, you can ensure that the products you offer meet or exceed customer expectations. Providing high-quality t-shirts that fit well enhances customer satisfaction, encourages repeat purchases, and contributes to the success of your print-on-demand business.

4.3 Finding Reliable T-Shirt Suppliers

Finding reliable t-shirt suppliers is crucial for the success of your print-on-demand (POD) business. Here are some steps to help you find trustworthy and high-quality t-shirt suppliers:

Research and Referrals: Start by conducting thorough research online and seeking recommendations from industry peers, fellow entrepreneurs, or POD communities. Look for suppliers with positive reviews, a good reputation, and a track record of delivering quality products on time.

Trade Shows and Events: Attend trade shows, industry events, and exhibitions related to the apparel and printing industry. These events provide opportunities to connect with suppliers, see their product samples firsthand, and discuss your requirements face-to-face. It allows you to establish personal relationships and evaluate the supplier's professionalism and product offerings.

Supplier Directories: Utilize online supplier directories like Alibaba, Thomasnet, or Sourcify. These directories provide comprehensive listings of suppliers across various industries, including apparel. Use filters and search functions to narrow down your options based on location, product type, and other criteria.

Request Samples: Once you have shortlisted potential suppliers, request samples of their t-shirts. This allows you to assess the quality of the fabric, stitching, printability, and overall craftsmanship. Evaluate the samples for comfort, durability, and whether they meet your specific requirements.

Quality Certifications: Inquire about the supplier's quality control measures and any relevant certifications they hold. Look for certifications such as ISO 9001, which indicate adherence to quality management standards. Certifications can be an assurance of a supplier's commitment to delivering high-quality products.

Production Capacity and Lead Times: Evaluate the supplier's production capacity and lead times. Ensure they can handle the volume of orders you anticipate, and that their production timelines align with your business requirements. Prompt and reliable fulfillment is crucial for maintaining customer satisfaction.

Communication and Responsiveness: Pay attention to the supplier's communication style and responsiveness during your interactions. Clear and prompt communication is essential for addressing any queries, discussing customization options, and ensuring a smooth collaboration.

Pricing and Terms: Compare pricing structures and payment terms offered by different suppliers. Keep in mind that the cheapest option may not always be the best in terms of quality and reliability. Balance the price with the value provided and consider any additional services or guarantees offered.

Flexibility and Customization: Assess the supplier's flexibility and willingness to accommodate customization requests. If you plan to offer unique designs or branding elements, ensure the supplier can accommodate custom printing, labeling, or packaging options.

References and Due Diligence: Request references from the supplier's existing clients or ask for testimonials from previous customers. Contact these references to gather insights on their experiences with the supplier, including product quality, service, and reliability.

Remember to document your interactions, compare the pros and cons of different suppliers, and make an informed decision based on your specific business needs. Building a strong and reliable partnership with your t-shirt supplier is crucial for maintaining the quality and consistency of your print-on-demand products.

4.4 Managing Inventory and Stock Levels

Managing inventory and stock levels is a crucial aspect of running a successful print-on-demand (POD) business. Since POD operates on a made-to-order model, inventory management is different compared to traditional retail businesses. Here are some key considerations for effectively managing inventory and stock levels in a print-on-demand setup:

Demand Forecasting: Analyze historical sales data, market trends, and customer preferences to forecast demand for your products. This helps you estimate the quantities of each design and size that are likely to sell, allowing you to adjust your production and stock levels accordingly.

Just-in-Time Manufacturing: With print-on-demand, you don't need to hold large quantities of pre-printed inventory. Instead, focus on implementing a just-in-time manufacturing approach, where you produce items as they are ordered. This minimizes the risk of excess inventory and reduces storage costs.

Supplier Relationships: Maintain a strong relationship with your print-on-demand production partners or suppliers. Ensure they have the capacity to handle your order volumes and can provide quick turnaround times. Regularly communicate with them to discuss production schedules, any upcoming promotions or sales, and any changes in demand.

Real-Time Inventory Monitoring: Utilize inventory management software or tools to track your stock levels in real-time. This allows you to have an accurate view of your inventory and helps you avoid stockouts or overstocking. Set up automated alerts for low stock levels to prompt timely reordering.

Print-on-Demand Integration: Integrate your print-on-demand platform or website with your inventory management system. This enables seamless synchronization of orders and inventory, ensuring accurate stock level updates and minimizing the risk of overselling.

Safety Stock: Maintain a safety stock level to account for unexpected fluctuations in demand or production delays. This buffer stock helps prevent stockouts and ensures you can fulfill orders promptly even during peak periods or unforeseen circumstances.

Analyze Sales and Trends: Regularly analyze sales data and monitor customer preferences and trends. Identify your best-selling designs, sizes, and variations to optimize your inventory management. This information can help you make informed decisions about which products to prioritize and which ones may need adjustments.

Seasonal and Trend Considerations: Take into account seasonal fluctuations and design trends when managing your inventory. Adjust your stock levels accordingly to meet customer demands during specific seasons or capitalize on popular design themes. This helps prevent excess inventory during off-peak periods.

Reordering and Production Lead Times: Maintain a clear understanding of the lead times required for production and restocking. Keep in mind any upcoming promotions or events that may impact order volumes. Place reorders in a timely manner to ensure a continuous supply of popular designs and sizes.

Returns and Exchanges: Implement a streamlined process for managing returns and exchanges. Ensure you have policies and procedures in place for handling and restocking returned items. This helps maintain accurate inventory levels and minimizes the impact of returns on your overall stock management.

Effective inventory management in a print-on-demand business requires a balance between maintaining sufficient stock levels to meet customer demand and minimizing excess inventory. By implementing the right tools, forecasting demand accurately, and staying informed about market trends, you can optimize your inventory and stock levels, ensuring a smooth and efficient print-on-demand operation.

Integrating with Print-on-Demand Platforms

5.1 Exploring Popular Print-on-Demand Services

Exploring popular print-on-demand (POD) services is an important step in setting up your POD business. These services provide the infrastructure, tools, and resources to help you create, sell, and fulfill custom products. Here are some well-known print-on-demand platforms worth exploring:

Printful: Printful is one of the leading print-on-demand services, offering a wide range of products such as t-shirts, hoodies, mugs, and more. They integrate with popular e-commerce platforms like Shopify, WooCommerce, and Etsy, making it easy to set up your online store. Printful handles printing, packaging, and shipping, allowing you to focus on designing and marketing your products.

Printify: Printify is another popular print-on-demand platform that connects you with a network of print providers. They offer a diverse range of customizable products and integrate with multiple e-commerce platforms. Printify enables you to choose the best print provider based on factors like pricing, location, and shipping times, providing flexibility and competitive pricing.

Gooten: Gooten offers a wide variety of print-on-demand products, including apparel, home decor, and accessories. They have a user-friendly interface and integrate with major e-commerce platforms. Gooten also provides a range of customization options and competitive pricing, along with global fulfillment and shipping capabilities.

Redbubble: Redbubble is a popular POD marketplace that allows independent artists and designers to sell their artwork on various products. It offers a wide range of products, including clothing, home decor, stationery, and more. Artists upload their designs, and

Redbubble handles printing, shipping, and customer service. It provides a built-in audience and community of art enthusiasts.

Society6: Society6 is another POD marketplace focused on promoting artwork and designs. Artists can upload their designs, which are then printed on various products like art prints, home decor, apparel, and accessories. Society6 takes care of the production, fulfillment, and customer service, allowing artists to showcase and sell their work.

Teespring: Teespring is a popular print-on-demand platform specifically focused on custom apparel. It allows you to design and sell t-shirts, hoodies, and other clothing items. Teespring offers a range of customization options, including the ability to create campaigns and promote your products through their built-in marketing features.

Merch by Amazon: Merch by Amazon is a POD service that allows you to create and sell custom t-shirts through the Amazon marketplace. You upload your designs, and Amazon handles the printing, fulfillment, and customer service. Merch by Amazon provides access to a massive customer base and takes care of order processing and shipping logistics.

When exploring print-on-demand services, consider factors such as product selection, integration capabilities, pricing, fulfillment options, customer service, and the platform's user experience. It's also important to review the terms and conditions, fees, and profit margins offered by each service. Take the time to compare and evaluate multiple platforms to find the one that best aligns with your business goals and requirements.

5.2 Uploading Your Designs to the Platform

Uploading your designs to a print-on-demand platform is a crucial step in starting your print-on-demand business. It allows you to showcase your unique designs and make them available for customers to purchase on various products. Here are the general steps involved in uploading your designs to a print-on-demand platform:

Create High-Quality Design Files: Before uploading your designs, ensure they are of high quality and meet the platform's specifications. Use professional design software like Adobe Photoshop or Illustrator to create your designs in the appropriate file format (e.g., JPEG, PNG, SVG) and at the recommended resolution and dimensions.

Prepare Multiple Design Variations: Consider creating different variations of your designs to cater to different products or customer preferences. For example, you may need separate design files for t-shirts, hoodies, mugs, and other items. Adapt your designs accordingly to ensure they look their best on each product type.

Choose the Print-on-Demand Platform: Select the print-on-demand platform or platforms where you want to upload your designs. Consider factors such as their popularity, user base, product range, integration options, and any specific features or benefits they offer. Research and compare multiple platforms to find the one that aligns with your business goals.

Sign Up and Set Up Your Account: Create an account on the chosen print-on-demand platform. Follow the registration process and provide the required information. Some platforms may require additional steps such as verifying your identity or linking your bank account for payment processing.

Navigate to the Design Upload Section: Once your account is set up, navigate to the design upload section or the product creation area on the platform. This is usually a dedicated area where you can add and manage your design files.

Select the Product and Design Placement: Choose the product or products you want to add your design to. It could be t-shirts, hoodies, phone cases, mugs, or any other available options. Specify the design placement, such as the front, back, sleeve, or all-over print, depending on the platform's capabilities.

Upload and Position Your Design: Use the platform's design upload tool to select and upload your design files. Depending on the platform, you may be able to adjust the size, rotation, and positioning of your design on the product mockup. Follow the platform's guidelines and recommendations for optimal design placement.

Preview and Customize Product Options: Review the product mockup with your design applied. Some platforms allow you to customize additional options like color variants, product variants (e.g., different sizes), or add text or other elements to complement your design. Take advantage of these customization features to enhance your product offerings.

Provide Product Descriptions and Tags: Write compelling and accurate product descriptions for each design and product combination. Use keywords and tags that are relevant to your design, target audience, and niche. This helps customers find your products through search engines or within the platform's marketplace.

Save and Publish Your Designs: Once you are satisfied with the design placement, customization options, and product descriptions, save and publish your designs. This makes them available for customers to purchase on the platform. Remember to review your uploaded designs periodically and make any necessary updates or additions as needed.

It's important to familiarize yourself with the specific design upload process and requirements of the print-on-demand platform you choose. Each platform may have its own interface, guidelines, and file format specifications. By carefully following the platform's instructions and optimizing your design presentations, you can effectively showcase your designs and attract potential customers to your print-on-demand products.

5.3 Customizing T-Shirt Options and Variants

Customizing t-shirt options and variants is an important aspect of offering a diverse range of products to your customers in the print-on-demand (POD) business. By providing various options, you can cater to different preferences, sizes, and styles. Here are some key considerations for customizing t-shirt options and variants:

T-Shirt Styles: Choose a range of t-shirt styles to offer to your customers. This could include basic crew neck t-shirts, V-neck t-shirts, tank tops, long-sleeve shirts, or even specialized styles like raglan sleeves or crop tops. Consider the popularity and demand for each style within your target audience.

Sizes and Fit: Offer a wide range of sizes to accommodate different body types and preferences. Include options for both men and women, as well as unisex or gender-neutral sizes. Typical size ranges may include small, medium, large, extra-large, and plus sizes. Ensure that the size options are clearly communicated to customers.

Color Variants: Provide a variety of color options for your t-shirts. Consider offering both classic colors like black, white, gray, and navy, as well as vibrant or trendy colors that align with your target audience's preferences. Keep in mind that certain colors may work better with specific designs, so choose a palette that complements your artwork.

Fabric Quality: Select high-quality t-shirt fabrics that offer comfort, durability, and a good printing surface. Common fabric options for t-shirts include cotton, polyester, or blends of the two. Consider the preferences of your target audience and ensure that the fabric you choose matches their expectations.

Custom Labels and Tags: Consider adding custom labels or tags to your t-shirts. These can include your brand logo, care instructions, or any other relevant information. Custom labels can enhance the perceived value of your products and contribute to a more professional and branded presentation.

Print Placement Options: Offer different print placement options for your designs. This can include front prints, back prints, sleeve prints, or all-over prints. Providing multiple placement options allows customers to choose the style that resonates with them the most. Ensure that your design files are prepared and sized appropriately for each print placement option.

Design Variations: Adapt your designs to suit different t-shirt options and variants. Consider how your design will appear on different styles, sizes, and colors. Adjust your artwork, layout, or color choices if needed to ensure the best visual impact on each t-shirt variant.

Personalization and Custom Requests: Explore options for personalization or custom requests. Some customers may want to add their names, initials, or specific messages to their t-shirts. Consider offering customization features that allow customers to add personalized elements to the design or request specific modifications.

Pricing Structure: Adjust your pricing based on the t-shirt options and variants you offer. Consider the cost of each option, including any premium fabrics, additional customization features, or specialized printing techniques. Ensure that your pricing reflects the value provided by each variant while remaining competitive in the market.

Customer Feedback and Market Trends: Continuously gather feedback from your customers and monitor market trends. Pay attention to the preferences and demands of your target audience and adjust your t-shirt options and variants accordingly. Stay updated with emerging styles, popular colors, and evolving customer preferences to stay ahead in the market.

Customizing t-shirt options and variants allows you to offer a diverse and appealing product selection to your customers. By understanding their preferences, adapting your designs, and considering the latest trends, you can create a compelling and personalized shopping experience that sets your print-on-demand business apart.

5.4 Pricing and Profit Margin Considerations

Pricing and profit margin considerations are essential for running a successful print-on-demand (POD) business. Setting the right prices ensures that your business remains profitable while offering competitive prices to attract customers. Here are some key factors to consider when determining pricing and profit margins:

Cost of Goods Sold (COGS): Calculate the cost of producing each item, including printing, materials, packaging, and any applicable fees charged by the print-on-demand platform. Consider the base cost of the product, customization options, and any additional features that may impact the production cost.

Platform Fees and Commissions: Take into account the fees and commissions charged by the print-on-demand platform for each sale. These can include transaction fees, listing fees, and a percentage of the sale price. Factor in these costs to ensure that your profit margins remain viable.

Target Profit Margin: Determine your desired profit margin for each product. This margin represents the amount you aim to earn after deducting the COGS and platform fees from the selling price. Consider industry standards, market competition, and your business goals when setting the profit margin.

Market Research and Competitive Analysis: Conduct thorough market research and analyze the pricing strategies of your competitors. Understand the average price range for similar products in your niche. While pricing competitively is important, also consider the value and uniqueness of your designs to justify a higher price point.

Value Perception: Consider how customers perceive the value of your products. Factors such as design quality, brand reputation, and customer reviews can influence the perceived value and justify higher pricing. Ensure that your prices align with the perceived value you offer to customers.

Pricing Strategies: Explore different pricing strategies based on your business objectives. These can include premium pricing for exclusive or limited edition designs, promotional pricing for new product launches or seasonal sales, or bundle pricing for offering discounts on multiple items.

Volume and Sales Forecasts: Analyze your sales forecasts and consider the potential volume of orders. Higher sales volume can allow for lower profit margins while still generating substantial revenue. Balance your profit margin goals with your sales projections to find the optimal pricing strategy.

Customer Acquisition and Retention: Factor in customer acquisition and retention costs when setting prices. If you invest in marketing, advertising, or other customer acquisition strategies, consider these expenses as part of your pricing strategy. Additionally, consider the potential lifetime value of customers and the importance of repeat purchases.

Pricing Adjustments: Regularly evaluate your pricing strategy based on market trends, customer feedback, and profitability analysis. Monitor sales performance, adjust prices as needed, and be flexible in response to changes in the market or customer demands.

Test and Iterate: Experiment with different pricing models, product bundles, or pricing tiers to determine what resonates best with your target audience. Conduct A/B testing or gather feedback from customers to gather insights and optimize your pricing strategy.

Finding the right balance between profitability and competitiveness is crucial for your print-on-demand business. Consider all the cost factors, profit margin goals, market dynamics, and customer perceptions when setting your prices. Regularly review and adjust your pricing strategy to ensure that it aligns with your business objectives and maximizes your profitability in the long term.

Marketing and Promoting Your Print-on-Demand T-Shirts

6.1 Building an Online Presence and Brand Identity

Building an online presence and establishing a strong brand identity is crucial for the success of your print-on-demand (POD) business. It helps you attract and engage with your target audience, differentiate yourself from competitors, and build customer loyalty. Here are some key steps to consider when building your online presence and brand identity:

Define Your Brand Identity: Start by defining your brand identity, including your brand values, mission, and unique selling proposition. Consider what sets your POD business apart and how you want to be perceived by your target audience. This will serve as the foundation for your brand's messaging and visual elements.

Develop a Brand Logo and Visual Identity: Create a distinctive brand logo and visual identity that aligns with your brand identity. This includes selecting colors, fonts, and design elements that reflect your brand's personality. Consistency in your visual identity across your website, social media profiles, and marketing materials helps in building brand recognition.

Build a Professional Website: Create a professional and user-friendly website that showcases your products, communicates your brand story, and makes it easy for customers to browse and purchase. Optimize your website for mobile devices, as a significant portion of online traffic comes from mobile users.

Optimize for Search Engines: Implement search engine optimization (SEO) strategies to improve your website's visibility in search engine results. Conduct keyword research to identify relevant search terms for your niche and incorporate them into your website content, including product descriptions, blog posts, and meta tags.

Content Marketing and Blogging: Create valuable and engaging content related to your niche through blog posts, articles, or videos. Share informative content, product guides, styling tips, or industry insights that resonate with your target audience. This positions you as an authority in your field and helps attract organic traffic to your website.

Social Media Presence: Establish a presence on relevant social media platforms where your target audience is active. Share visually appealing images of your products, behind-the-scenes content, customer testimonials, and engage with your audience through comments and direct messages. Consistency in your brand voice and messaging across social media channels is key.

Influencer Collaborations: Collaborate with influencers or micro-influencers in your niche to promote your products and expand your reach. Identify influencers who align with your brand values and have an engaged following. Their endorsement can help increase brand visibility and credibility.

Email Marketing: Build an email list and utilize email marketing to nurture relationships with your customers. Offer incentives, such as exclusive discounts or early access to new designs, to encourage sign-ups. Send regular newsletters with updates, promotions, and personalized recommendations to keep customers engaged and encourage repeat purchases.

Customer Engagement and Support: Provide excellent customer support and actively engage with your customers. Respond to inquiries promptly, address concerns, and show appreciation for their support. Encourage customer reviews and testimonials to build trust and social proof.

Analytics and Data Tracking: Utilize analytics tools to track website traffic, customer behavior, and sales data. Analyze the data to identify trends, understand customer preferences, and make data-driven decisions to optimize your marketing efforts and product offerings.

Consistency, authenticity, and value are key when building an online presence and brand identity. Continuously monitor your online channels, adapt to customer feedback, and evolve your brand strategy to stay relevant and connected with your target audience.

6.2 Leveraging Social Media for Promotion

Leveraging social media for promotion is an effective way to increase brand awareness, drive traffic to your print-on-demand (POD) store, and engage with your target audience. Here are some strategies for effectively using social media for promotion:

Choose the Right Platforms: Identify the social media platforms where your target audience is most active. Common platforms for promoting POD products include Instagram, Facebook, Pinterest, and Twitter. Focus on platforms that align with your brand and allow you to showcase your products visually.

Create Compelling Visual Content: Visuals are crucial in the world of social media. Invest in high-quality product photography and graphic design to create visually appealing content that grabs attention. Showcase your products in creative and engaging ways, highlighting their unique features and benefits.

Build a Consistent Brand Presence: Maintain a consistent brand presence across your social media profiles. Use your brand logo, colors, and visual identity consistently to enhance brand recognition. Craft a compelling bio or "About" section that clearly communicates your brand values, mission, and what sets your POD business apart.

Engage with Your Audience: Actively engage with your followers and customers. Respond to comments, messages, and inquiries in a timely and friendly manner. Encourage conversations, ask questions, and seek feedback to foster a sense of community and build relationships with your audience.

Use Hashtags Strategically: Research relevant hashtags and use them in your social media posts to increase discoverability. Hashtags help users interested in specific topics find your content. Create a branded hashtag for your POD business to encourage user-generated content and make it easier for customers to share their purchases.

Run Contests and Giveaways: Engage your audience by running contests or giveaways on social media. Encourage participants to share your content, tag friends, or follow your page to enter. This helps increase brand reach, generates excitement, and drives engagement.

Collaborate with Influencers: Partner with influencers or micro-influencers in your niche who have a following that aligns with your target audience. Collaborations can include sponsored posts, product reviews, or giveaways. Influencers can introduce your brand to their audience and help build credibility and trust.

Share User-Generated Content: Encourage customers to share photos of themselves wearing or using your POD products. Repost and share user-generated content, giving credit to the original creator. User-generated content serves as social proof and helps showcase your products in real-life situations.

Utilize Social Ads: Consider running paid social media advertising campaigns to reach a wider audience and drive targeted traffic to your store. Platforms like Facebook and Instagram offer sophisticated targeting options, allowing you to reach specific demographics or interests.

Monitor and Analyze Performance: Regularly monitor your social media performance using analytics tools provided by each platform. Track metrics such as engagement, reach, click-through rates, and conversions. Analyze the data to understand what content resonates best with your audience and adjust your strategy accordingly.

Remember that social media promotion is about building relationships, fostering engagement, and providing value to your audience. Be authentic, consistent, and responsive in your approach to establish a strong online presence and maximize the promotion of your print-on-demand products.

6.3 Implementing Effective Marketing Strategies

Implementing effective marketing strategies is essential for driving traffic, increasing conversions, and growing your print-on-demand (POD) business. Here are some key strategies to consider:

Define Your Target Audience: Clearly identify your target audience and understand their demographics, interests, and purchasing behavior. This will help you tailor your marketing messages and reach the right people with your promotions.

Content Marketing: Create valuable and relevant content that educates, entertains, or inspires your audience. Blog posts, videos, tutorials, or infographics can help showcase your expertise, attract organic traffic, and build trust with potential customers.

Search Engine Optimization (SEO): Optimize your website and content for search engines to increase organic visibility. Conduct keyword research to understand what terms your target audience is searching for and optimize your product descriptions, blog posts, and other content accordingly.

Email Marketing: Build an email list and leverage email marketing to nurture relationships with your audience. Send regular newsletters, product updates, exclusive discounts, and personalized recommendations to engage customers and encourage repeat purchases.

Social Media Marketing: Utilize social media platforms to showcase your products, engage with your audience, and drive traffic to your POD store. Create visually appealing content, interact with followers, collaborate with influencers, and run targeted ad campaigns to increase brand visibility and attract customers.

Influencer Marketing: Collaborate with influencers or micro-influencers in your niche to promote your products. Partner with influencers who align with your brand values and have an engaged following. Their endorsement can increase brand exposure and drive conversions.

Paid Advertising: Consider running paid advertising campaigns on platforms like Google Ads or social media channels to reach a wider audience. Set clear campaign objectives, target specific demographics or interests, and optimize your ads based on performance data.

Affiliate Marketing: Establish an affiliate program where influencers, bloggers, or brand advocates earn a commission for promoting and driving sales to your POD store. This can help expand your reach and leverage the influence of others to generate sales.

Remarketing and Retargeting: Implement remarketing campaigns to target people who have previously visited your website or shown interest in your products. By displaying tailored ads to these users across various platforms, you can increase brand recall and encourage them to complete a purchase.

Analytics and Testing: Regularly monitor and analyze marketing performance using analytics tools. Track metrics such as website traffic, conversion rates, customer acquisition costs, and customer lifetime value. Test different strategies, messaging, and channels to optimize your marketing efforts based on data-driven insights.

Remember, effective marketing is an ongoing process that requires experimentation, adaptation, and continuous improvement. Stay informed about industry trends, monitor customer feedback, and be willing to adjust your strategies to meet the evolving needs of your target audience.

6.4 Collaborating with Influencers and Affiliates

Collaborating with influencers and affiliates can be a powerful strategy to promote your print-on-demand (POD) products and expand your reach. Here's a breakdown of how to effectively collaborate with influencers and affiliates:

Identify Relevant Influencers: Look for influencers who align with your brand values, target audience, and niche. Consider their follower demographics, engagement rates, and the type of content they produce. Ensure that their audience matches your target market to maximize the impact of the collaboration.

Reach Out to Influencers: Contact influencers through email, direct messages, or influencer marketing platforms. Personalize your outreach by highlighting why you believe their partnership would be valuable. Offer incentives such as free products, exclusive discounts, or commission-based collaborations.

Set Clear Expectations: Clearly communicate your expectations, objectives, and guidelines for the collaboration. Specify the type of content you would like them to create, the messaging you want them to convey, and any specific hashtags or brand mentions to include. Provide them with product samples or access to your POD platform as needed.

Track Performance and Metrics: Establish key performance indicators (KPIs) to measure the success of the influencer collaboration. Track metrics such as engagement rates, reach, conversions, or coupon code usage. Monitor the impact on website traffic, sales, and brand awareness. This data will help you evaluate the effectiveness of each collaboration.

Affiliate Program: Create an affiliate program to incentivize individuals to promote your POD products. Affiliates earn a commission for each sale they generate through their unique referral links or coupon codes. Provide them with promotional materials, tracking tools, and support to maximize their effectiveness.

Provide Collaborative Assets: Offer influencers and affiliates high-quality visuals, product descriptions, and promotional materials that align with your brand's style and messaging. This makes it easier for them to create content that showcases your products effectively and consistently.

Monitor and Engage: Regularly monitor the content created by influencers and affiliates, and engage with their posts and their followers. Like, comment, and share their content to extend its reach and demonstrate your appreciation for their efforts. This engagement fosters a positive relationship and encourages them to continue promoting your products.

Measure ROI: Evaluate the return on investment (ROI) for each influencer and affiliate collaboration. Assess the sales generated, cost per acquisition, brand exposure, and the overall impact on your business. Adjust your strategies based on the performance of each collaboration to optimize future partnerships.

Long-term Relationships: Nurture long-term relationships with influencers and affiliates who consistently drive positive results. Maintain open communication, provide ongoing support, and explore opportunities for additional collaborations or exclusive partnerships. Building strong relationships can lead to sustained brand advocacy and loyalty.

Compliance with Guidelines: Ensure that influencers and affiliates comply with relevant advertising and disclosure guidelines. Familiarize yourself with the guidelines specific to your region or platform to avoid any legal or ethical issues. Transparency builds trust with your audience and safeguards your brand's reputation.

Collaborating with influencers and affiliates can amplify your brand's visibility, reach new audiences, and drive sales for your POD business. By selecting the right partners, setting clear expectations, and nurturing relationships, you can leverage their influence and expertise to achieve your marketing goals.

Managing Orders and Customer Service

7.1 Handling Incoming Orders and Fulfillment

Handling incoming orders and fulfillment is a critical aspect of running a print-on-demand (POD) business. It involves efficiently processing orders, managing inventory, and ensuring timely delivery to customers. Here's an overview of the steps involved in handling incoming orders and fulfillment for your POD business:

Order Management System: Implement an order management system or utilize the features provided by your chosen POD platform to efficiently manage incoming orders. This system should track order details, customer information, and payment processing.

Automated Order Processing: Set up automated processes for order fulfillment to streamline the workflow. When an order is placed, it should be automatically sent to your chosen POD supplier for production.

Production and Printing: Coordinate with your POD supplier to ensure they have the necessary information and files to fulfill each order. Provide clear specifications for printing, including design, colors, sizes, and any additional customization options.

Quality Control: Maintain quality control standards to ensure that each product meets your brand's expectations. Regularly inspect samples and perform quality checks on completed orders to maintain consistency and customer satisfaction.

Packaging and Branding: Determine your packaging materials and branding elements to create a positive unboxing experience for customers. Consider including personalized thank-you notes, promotional materials, or other branded touches to enhance customer satisfaction and brand loyalty.

Shipping and Delivery: Choose reliable shipping carriers or fulfillment services to handle the delivery of your products. Ensure that you have accurate shipping rates configured within your e-commerce platform to provide transparent pricing for customers. Communicate tracking information to customers so they can monitor the progress of their shipments.

Inventory Management: Keep track of your inventory levels to avoid stockouts or overselling. Monitor product availability and replenish stock as needed to fulfill incoming orders. Regularly assess sales trends and adjust your inventory levels accordingly to optimize your supply chain.

Order Status and Customer Communication: Establish clear communication channels to keep customers informed about the status of their orders. Provide order confirmation emails, shipping notifications, and tracking information to enhance transparency and customer satisfaction. Promptly address any customer inquiries or concerns related to their orders.

Returns and Exchanges: Establish a returns and exchanges policy that is fair and customer-friendly. Clearly communicate the process and requirements for returns or exchanges on your website. Promptly handle return requests and provide refunds or replacements as necessary to maintain customer satisfaction.

Customer Feedback and Reviews: Encourage customers to leave feedback and reviews about their purchase experience. Monitor and respond to reviews promptly, whether positive or negative, to show your dedication to customer satisfaction and address any concerns publicly.

Efficient order management and fulfillment processes are essential to provide a positive customer experience and maintain a good reputation for your POD business. Regularly review and optimize your workflows to ensure smooth operations and timely order processing.

7.2 Ensuring Quality Control and Packaging

Ensuring quality control and packaging is crucial for maintaining customer satisfaction and delivering a positive experience with your print-on-demand (POD) products. Here are some key considerations for ensuring quality control and effective packaging:

Quality Control Processes: Implement quality control measures to maintain consistent product standards. This involves inspecting samples, conducting quality checks during production, and performing post-production inspections. Monitor the print quality, color accuracy, fabric or material integrity, and any customization details to ensure that each product meets your brand's standards.

Clear Production Guidelines: Provide clear and detailed production guidelines to your POD supplier or production team. Specify design requirements, color profiles, preferred file formats, and any other specifications necessary for accurate and high-quality printing. Clearly communicate your expectations to minimize errors and ensure consistency across orders.

Sample Testing: Request and evaluate product samples from your POD supplier to assess the quality before launching your products. This allows you to identify any potential issues or areas for improvement in terms of print quality, fabric feel, sizing, or overall product construction.

Packaging Materials: Choose appropriate packaging materials that provide sufficient protection during shipping while reflecting your brand's image. Consider using durable polybags, bubble mailers, or boxes that prevent damage to the product during transit. Additionally, select packaging materials that align with your brand's sustainability goals, such as using recyclable or biodegradable options.

Branding and Presentation: Use packaging as an opportunity to reinforce your brand identity. Consider including custom branding elements such as logo stickers, tissue paper, or branded packaging inserts. These small touches enhance the unboxing experience and leave a lasting impression on customers.

Secure Packaging: Ensure that your products are packaged securely to prevent damage during transportation. Use appropriate padding, such as bubble wrap or tissue paper, to protect delicate items or prints. Consider using inserts or dividers to keep multiple items organized and prevent them from shifting during transit.

Clear Product Labels and Information: Include clear and accurate product labels on the packaging. This may include product names, SKU or barcode information, sizing, care instructions, and any relevant legal or safety information. Clear labeling helps customers identify and handle the products appropriately.

Quality Assurance Checks: Conduct random quality assurance checks on packaged products before shipping them to customers. This step involves verifying that the correct items are included, checking for any defects or damage, and ensuring that all packaging elements are in place.

Shipping Method Selection: Choose reliable shipping carriers or fulfillment services that prioritize safe and timely delivery. Research shipping options to find those that offer tracking, insurance, and reliable handling to minimize the risk of product damage or loss during transit.

Customer Feedback and Returns: Encourage customers to provide feedback on the packaging and product quality. Monitor customer reviews and address any concerns promptly. If a customer receives a damaged or defective product, have a clear returns or exchange policy in place to offer a resolution and maintain customer satisfaction.

By prioritizing quality control and thoughtful packaging, you can ensure that customers receive products that meet their expectations and create a positive impression of your brand. Regularly review and refine your quality control processes and packaging strategies to optimize the customer experience and uphold your brand's reputation.

7.3 Providing Excellent Customer Service

Providing excellent customer service is vital for the success of your print-on-demand (POD) business. It helps build trust, foster customer loyalty, and drive positive word-of-mouth referrals. Here are some key considerations for providing excellent customer service in the context of print on demand:

Prompt and Responsive Communication: Respond to customer inquiries, concerns, or feedback promptly. Aim to provide timely and helpful responses via various communication channels such as email, live chat, or social media. Ensure that your customer service team is accessible and knowledgeable about your products, processes, and policies.

Clear and Transparent Policies: Clearly communicate your policies regarding shipping, returns, exchanges, and refunds. Make these policies easily accessible on your website or within the ordering process. Provide detailed information about shipping timeframes, conditions for returns or exchanges, and any associated fees. Transparent policies build trust and set customer expectations.

Personalized Support: Offer personalized assistance to customers whenever possible. Address customers by name, listen actively to their concerns, and provide tailored solutions to their inquiries or issues. Demonstrating a personal touch shows that you value their business and are dedicated to their satisfaction.

Proactive Order Updates: Keep customers informed about the status of their orders. Send automated order confirmations, shipping notifications, and tracking information to provide transparency and peace of mind. Proactively communicate any delays or issues with their orders and offer solutions or alternatives when necessary.

Flexibility and Problem Resolution: Be flexible and accommodating when resolving customer issues. If a customer encounters a problem with their order, offer solutions such as replacements, refunds, or discounts. Empower your customer service team to handle such situations and ensure they have the necessary authority to resolve problems promptly.

Product Knowledge and Expertise: Train your customer service team to have in-depth knowledge about your products, design options, sizing, and customization features. This enables them to provide accurate information, make recommendations, and address customer queries effectively.

Continuous Improvement: Regularly evaluate customer feedback and identify areas for improvement. Analyze customer reviews, surveys, and support interactions to identify recurring issues or pain points. Use this information to refine your processes, enhance product offerings, and improve the overall customer experience.

Professional and Courteous Tone: Maintain a professional and courteous tone in all customer interactions. Use respectful language, be patient, and empathize with customers' concerns. Avoid confrontations or arguments and focus on finding solutions to their problems.

Customer Feedback and Reviews: Encourage customers to provide feedback and reviews about their experience with your products and customer service. Monitor and respond to reviews promptly, whether positive or negative, to show your commitment to customer satisfaction and address any concerns publicly.

Employee Training and Empowerment: Invest in training your customer service team on product knowledge, communication skills, and problem-solving techniques. Empower them to make decisions and resolve issues independently. Foster a positive and supportive work environment that values excellent customer service.

Remember, providing excellent customer service requires ongoing commitment and attention. By prioritizing customer satisfaction, you can build a loyal customer base and differentiate your POD business from competitors in the market.

7.4 Dealing with Returns and Exchanges

Dealing with returns and exchanges is an important aspect of managing a print-on-demand (POD) business. It's essential to have clear policies and processes in place to handle customer requests effectively. Here's a step-by-step guide for dealing with returns and exchanges in a POD business:

Establish Return and Exchange Policies: Create clear and fair policies regarding returns and exchanges. Clearly outline the conditions under which returns or exchanges are accepted, such as damaged products, incorrect sizes, or printing errors. Specify the timeframe within which customers can initiate return or exchange requests.

Communicate Return and Exchange Procedures: Make the return and exchange procedures easily accessible to customers. Include them on your website, within order confirmation emails, or as a separate section in the customer support area. Provide detailed instructions on how customers can initiate a return or exchange, including the required information and any documentation they need to provide.

Provide a Return/Exchange Request Form: Offer a user-friendly return or exchange request form on your website. This form should collect essential information from the customer, such as order details, reason for return or exchange, and desired resolution. Streamline the form to make the process as simple as possible for the customer.

Assess Eligibility for Returns/Exchanges: Review the return or exchange requests based on your established policies. Verify if the customer meets the criteria for returning or exchanging the product, such as being within the specified timeframe and providing valid reasons. Evaluate the provided information and any accompanying evidence, such as photos of damaged products.

Communicate with the Customer: Maintain clear and prompt communication with the customer throughout the returns or exchanges process. Acknowledge their request and provide updates on the progress. If additional information or clarification is needed, reach out to the customer to gather the required details.

Provide Resolution Options: Once the return or exchange request is approved, offer resolution options to the customer. This may include providing a refund, sending a replacement product, or issuing store credit. Work with the customer to determine their preferred resolution and address any concerns they may have.

Arrange Product Return: If the customer needs to return the product, provide them with clear instructions on how to do so. Specify the return address and any specific packaging requirements. Consider offering prepaid return shipping labels or reimbursing the customer for return shipping costs, depending on your policies.

Inspect Returned Products: Upon receiving the returned product, inspect it to ensure it meets your criteria for a return or exchange. Check for any damage, signs of wear, or discrepancies with the customer's claim. This step ensures that you maintain quality control and prevents abuse of your return policy.

Process Refunds or Exchanges: Once the returned product is approved, proceed with issuing a refund or arranging for an exchange. Process refunds promptly according to your chosen payment gateway or method. If exchanging the product, confirm the customer's preferred size, design, or any other customization details.

Update Inventory and Fulfillment: Update your inventory levels accordingly based on the returned products or any new products required for exchanges. Coordinate with your POD supplier or production team to fulfill the replacement products promptly.

Continual Improvement: Regularly analyze the reasons for returns and exchanges to identify trends or recurring issues. Use this information to improve product quality, address common concerns, and refine your production or fulfillment processes.

By establishing clear policies, maintaining open communication, and efficiently managing returns and exchanges, you can provide a positive customer experience and build trust in your POD business. Continuous improvement based on customer feedback will help you reduce the number of returns and exchanges over time.

Analyzing Data and Scaling Your Business

8.1 Tracking Sales and Performance Metrics

Tracking sales and performance metrics is essential for monitoring the success and growth of your print-on-demand (POD) business. By analyzing key metrics, you can make data-driven decisions, identify areas for improvement, and measure the effectiveness of your marketing and sales strategies. Here are some important sales and performance metrics to track in a POD business:

Sales Revenue: Monitor your total sales revenue to understand the overall financial performance of your business. This metric helps you track the success of your product offerings and pricing strategies.

Order Volume: Keep track of the number of orders placed within a specific timeframe. This metric provides insights into the demand for your products and helps you identify peak seasons or trends.

Average Order Value (AOV): Calculate the average value of each order by dividing the total revenue by the number of orders. A higher AOV indicates that customers are purchasing more items or higher-priced products, which can impact your profitability.

Conversion Rate: Measure the percentage of website visitors who make a purchase. This metric helps you evaluate the effectiveness of your website design, product descriptions, and overall user experience.

Return Rate: Monitor the percentage of orders that are returned by customers. A high return rate may indicate product quality issues or customer dissatisfaction, highlighting areas for improvement.

Customer Acquisition Cost (CAC): Determine the cost incurred to acquire a new customer. This metric considers marketing and advertising expenses, divided by the number of new customers acquired. Tracking CAC helps you assess the efficiency of your customer acquisition strategies.

Customer Lifetime Value (CLV): Calculate the total value a customer brings to your business over their lifetime. This metric considers the average order value, purchase frequency, and customer retention rate. A high CLV indicates that customers are loyal and generate significant revenue for your business.

Repeat Purchase Rate: Measure the percentage of customers who make repeat purchases. This metric demonstrates customer loyalty and the effectiveness of your retention strategies. Encouraging repeat purchases can significantly impact your revenue and profitability.

Traffic Sources: Analyze the sources of website traffic, such as organic search, social media, paid ads, or referrals. This information helps you identify the most effective marketing channels and optimize your marketing efforts accordingly.

Social Media Engagement: Track metrics like the number of followers, likes, shares, and comments on social media platforms. These metrics indicate the level of engagement with your brand and can help you assess the impact of your social media marketing efforts.

Conversion Funnel Analysis: Analyze the different stages of your sales funnel, from website visitors to completed purchases. Identify potential drop-off points or areas of improvement to optimize your conversion rates.

Inventory Management: Monitor inventory levels to ensure you have sufficient stock to meet customer demand. Tracking inventory turnover rate and popular product variations can help you make informed decisions about restocking and expanding your product line.

Profit Margin: Calculate the profit margin for each product by subtracting the production and fulfillment costs from the selling price.

Tracking profit margin helps you understand the profitability of individual products and make pricing adjustments if needed.

Customer Satisfaction and Reviews: Monitor customer feedback, ratings, and reviews to gauge overall satisfaction. Positive reviews and high ratings indicate a strong brand reputation and customer loyalty.

To track these metrics effectively, use analytics tools like Google Analytics, e-commerce platforms' built-in reporting features, and customer relationship management (CRM) systems. Regularly review and analyze the data to identify trends, set goals, and make data-driven decisions to optimize your print-on-demand business's performance.

8.2 Identifying Trends and Customer Preferences

Identifying trends and understanding customer preferences is crucial for the success of your print-on-demand (POD) business. By staying updated on market trends and knowing what customers are looking for, you can create designs that resonate with your target audience and drive sales. Here are some key steps to help you identify trends and customer preferences in the POD industry:

Research Market Trends: Stay informed about the latest trends in fashion, pop culture, and design. Monitor industry publications, fashion magazines, social media platforms, and trend forecasting websites. Look for patterns, themes, and emerging styles that align with your target audience.

Study Competitors: Analyze what your competitors are doing and the designs they are promoting. Explore their bestselling products, customer reviews, and social media engagement. Identify common themes, unique design elements, and customer preferences to gain insights into what is resonating with customers in your niche.

Analyze Customer Feedback: Pay attention to customer feedback, both positive and negative. Reviews, comments, and direct customer interactions can provide valuable insights into what customers like or dislike about your products. Look for common themes and suggestions for improvement to enhance your designs and offerings.

Conduct Surveys and Polls: Engage with your existing customers and potential target audience through surveys and polls. Ask them about their preferences, favorite design styles, colors, and trends they are interested in. This direct feedback can help you tailor your designs and products to their preferences.

Track Social Media Engagement: Monitor social media platforms to gauge customer reactions and engagement with various design styles and trends. Pay attention to the number of likes, comments, shares, and overall sentiment related to specific design elements or themes. This can help you identify popular trends and design aesthetics.

Monitor Sales and Product Performance: Analyze your sales data and product performance metrics to identify patterns and trends. Look for the designs, styles, or themes that generate the highest sales or receive positive customer feedback. This data can guide you in developing new designs that align with customer preferences.

Seek Inspiration from Influencers: Follow influencers and content creators in your niche or relevant industries. Observe their content, collaborations, and design choices. Influencers often have their finger on the pulse of current trends and can provide inspiration for your own designs.

Attend Trade Shows and Events: Participate in industry trade shows, exhibitions, and events where you can connect with suppliers, designers, and industry experts. These events offer opportunities to learn about the latest trends, network, and gain insights into customer preferences.

Stay Updated with Design Platforms and Tools: Explore design platforms, marketplaces, and print-on-demand service providers to understand the design styles and themes that are popular among customers. Many platforms showcase trending designs and offer insights into customer preferences.

Experiment and Iterate: Continuously experiment with new designs, styles, and themes to test customer responses. Launch limited-edition designs or run A/B tests to gauge customer interest. Use the feedback and sales data to refine your designs and offerings based on what resonates best with your target audience.

Remember, customer preferences and trends can change rapidly, so it's important to stay agile and adaptable. Regularly review and analyze the data and feedback you gather to stay ahead of evolving trends and meet the changing demands of your customers. By identifying and incorporating popular trends and customer preferences into your print-on-demand business, you can increase customer engagement, drive sales, and build a loyal customer base.

8.3 Expanding Product Offerings and Designs

Expanding your product offerings and designs is a great way to attract new customers, increase sales, and keep your print-on-demand (POD) business fresh and exciting. Here are some key steps to help you expand your product offerings and designs:

Analyze Customer Insights: Review customer feedback, purchase patterns, and market research to identify gaps in your current product offerings. Look for customer requests, popular design themes, or product categories that align with your target audience's preferences.

Identify New Product Opportunities: Explore different product categories beyond t-shirts, such as hoodies, tank tops, accessories, or home decor items. Consider the potential demand for these products and how they complement your existing designs and brand identity.

Research Market Trends: Stay updated on the latest market trends and design styles relevant to your target audience. Follow fashion trends, industry publications, design blogs, and social media platforms to identify emerging styles, patterns, colors, and themes that resonate with customers.

Collaborate with Artists and Designers: Partner with talented artists and designers to expand your design portfolio. Collaborations bring fresh perspectives and unique design aesthetics to your product offerings. Consider hosting design contests or reaching out to artists directly to establish partnerships.

Offer Personalization and Customization: Allow customers to personalize or customize their products. Offer options for text customization, color variations, or the ability to upload custom images or artwork. This adds a personal touch and increases customer engagement.

Conduct Market Testing: Test new product offerings and designs on a smaller scale before a full launch. Consider limited edition releases, pre-orders, or crowdfunding campaigns to gauge customer interest and validate the demand for new products.

Monitor Sales and Feedback: Track the performance of new products and designs using sales data, customer feedback, and reviews. Analyze the sales conversion rates, customer satisfaction, and return rates to assess the success of your expanded offerings.

Optimize Production and Fulfillment Processes: Ensure that your production and fulfillment processes can handle the increased product variety and volume. Coordinate with your POD provider or production team to ensure efficient manufacturing, quality control, and timely fulfillment of orders.

Leverage Seasonal and Holiday Themes: Capitalize on seasonal and holiday trends by creating designs that align with specific occasions or themes. This can help boost sales during peak periods and increase customer engagement.

Stay Creative and Innovative: Continually explore new design techniques, materials, and printing options to offer unique and innovative products. Experiment with different textures, printing methods, and finishing touches to make your designs stand out.

Seek Customer Input: Engage with your customers through surveys, polls, or social media to gather input on potential product expansions or design concepts. Consider their suggestions and preferences when planning your product roadmap.

Keep an Eye on Competition: Monitor your competitors' product offerings and design strategies. While it's important to differentiate yourself, understanding what works for others in your industry can provide valuable insights and inspiration.

Maintain Brand Consistency: Ensure that your expanded product offerings and designs align with your brand identity and target audience. Consistency in design aesthetic, quality, and messaging helps build brand recognition and customer loyalty.

Expanding your product offerings and designs requires a thoughtful approach that balances customer preferences, market trends, and your brand identity. Regularly assess the performance of new products, gather customer feedback, and make adjustments as necessary. By continuously expanding and evolving your offerings, you can attract a broader customer base, increase customer engagement, and drive long-term growth for your POD business.

8.4 Scaling Up Production and Outsourcing

Scaling up production is a crucial step in the growth of your print-on-demand (POD) business. As the demand for your products increases, you may need to explore outsourcing options to effectively manage the increased workload. Here are some key considerations for scaling up production and outsourcing in a print-on-demand business:

Assess Production Capacity: Evaluate your current production capacity and determine if it can meet the growing demand for your products. Consider factors such as equipment, printing capabilities, available resources, and manpower. Identify any limitations or bottlenecks that may hinder your ability to fulfill larger volumes of orders.

Identify Outsourcing Opportunities: Research and identify potential outsourcing partners or print-on-demand service providers that can handle the increased production volume. Look for reputable companies with experience in the POD industry, quality printing capabilities, and the ability to meet your specific requirements.

Quality Assurance: Ensure that any outsourcing partner you consider maintains high-quality standards and can produce products that meet your customers' expectations. Request samples or conduct a trial run to assess their printing quality, materials used, and overall product consistency.

Communication and Collaboration: Establish clear lines of communication with your outsourcing partner. Clearly communicate your brand guidelines, design specifications, and quality standards. Regularly communicate with them to address any concerns, provide feedback, and ensure a smooth production process.

Cost Considerations: Evaluate the costs associated with outsourcing versus in-house production. Compare the expenses of equipment, labor, materials, and shipping when making a decision. Keep in mind that outsourcing may provide cost savings in terms of equipment investment and staffing requirements.

Scalability and Flexibility: Choose an outsourcing partner that can scale up production as your business grows. Ensure they have the capacity to handle increased order volumes during peak seasons or promotional campaigns. Flexibility in production turnaround times is also essential to meet customer expectations.

Quality Control: Establish quality control procedures to maintain consistency and ensure that outsourced products meet your brand's quality standards. Develop clear guidelines, conduct periodic quality checks, and implement feedback mechanisms to address any issues promptly.

Logistics and Shipping: Consider the logistics and shipping arrangements when outsourcing production. Ensure that the outsourcing partner can handle order fulfillment, packaging, and timely delivery. Evaluate their shipping options, tracking capabilities, and return/exchange processes.

Intellectual Property Protection: Safeguard your designs and intellectual property when working with outsourcing partners. Implement confidentiality agreements, non-disclosure agreements, or trademarks to protect your brand's unique assets.

Monitor Performance: Continuously monitor the performance of your outsourcing partner in terms of quality, delivery times, and customer satisfaction. Regularly assess their ability to meet your requirements and address any concerns or issues that may arise.

Transitioning from In-house to Outsourcing: If you decide to transition from in-house production to outsourcing, plan the transition carefully. Gradually reduce in-house production while increasing the volume of outsourced orders to ensure a smooth transition without compromising quality or customer experience.

Risk Management: Have contingency plans in place to mitigate risks associated with outsourcing. This includes having alternative suppliers or outsourcing partners in case of unexpected disruptions, delays, or quality issues.

Remember, outsourcing production is a strategic decision that requires thorough research, due diligence, and ongoing management. Regularly evaluate the performance and effectiveness of your outsourcing arrangements to ensure they align with your business goals and customer expectations. By scaling up production and effectively outsourcing, you can efficiently meet customer demand, expand your business, and focus on other aspects of growing your print-on-demand business.

Troubleshooting and FAQs

9.1 Addressing Common Print-on-Demand Challenges

Print-on-demand (POD) businesses can face certain challenges that need to be addressed effectively to ensure smooth operations and customer satisfaction. Here are some common challenges in the print-on-demand industry and strategies to address them:

Quality Control: Maintaining consistent print quality is crucial for customer satisfaction. Work closely with your printing partners or POD service providers to establish clear quality standards, conduct regular quality checks, and provide feedback for improvement. Monitor customer feedback and address any quality issues promptly.

Order Fulfillment and Shipping: Timely order fulfillment and reliable shipping are essential for customer satisfaction. Streamline your order processing and fulfillment workflows, ensuring efficient communication between your store, printing partners, and shipping providers. Monitor shipping performance, offer tracking options, and provide responsive customer support for any shipping-related inquiries or issues.

Product Availability and Stock Management: Keep track of your inventory and ensure that popular products are always available. Implement inventory management systems or work closely with your POD service provider to maintain accurate stock levels. Consider pre-order or back-order options to manage demand during high-volume periods.

Communication and Customer Support: Prompt and effective communication is key to managing customer inquiries, concerns, and support requests. Provide clear channels for customer communication, including email, live chat, or social media platforms. Respond promptly to customer queries, provide regular updates on order status, and address any issues or complaints with empathy and professionalism.

Design Copyright and Intellectual Property: Protecting your designs and respecting copyright laws is vital. Ensure that your designs are original or properly licensed to avoid legal issues. Conduct thorough research and use reputable sources for design elements. Educate yourself on copyright laws and seek legal advice if needed.

Print File Preparation and Design Compatibility: Prepare your print files correctly to ensure compatibility with printing processes and equipment. Follow the guidelines provided by your POD service provider regarding file formats, resolution, color profiles, and bleed areas. Test print files before launching them to ensure accurate representation of your designs.

Pricing and Profit Margin Management: Set competitive and profitable pricing for your products. Consider factors such as production costs, shipping expenses, overheads, and desired profit margins. Regularly evaluate and adjust your pricing strategy based on market trends, competition, and customer feedback.

Managing Customer Expectations: Clearly communicate product descriptions, sizing charts, and any limitations or variations in printing processes to manage customer expectations effectively. Provide accurate product images and descriptions to minimize the chance of customers receiving products that differ from their expectations.

Returns and Refunds: Establish a clear returns and refunds policy to address customer dissatisfaction or product issues. Ensure that the process is customer-friendly and efficient. Analyze return reasons and patterns to identify potential areas for improvement in product quality, customer support, or design accuracy.

Keeping Up with Market Trends: Stay updated on industry trends, customer preferences, and emerging design styles. Regularly research and analyze market trends, competitor offerings, and customer feedback to adapt your product designs, styles, and marketing strategies accordingly.

Addressing these common challenges requires a combination of proactive planning, effective communication, ongoing monitoring, and continuous improvement. By staying vigilant and responsive, you can overcome these challenges and provide a positive experience for your customers, leading to long-term success in the print-on-demand industry.

9.2 Managing Customer Complaints and Issues

Managing customer complaints and issues effectively is crucial for maintaining a positive reputation and ensuring customer satisfaction in the print-on-demand (POD) business. Here are some key steps to help you handle customer complaints and issues:

Prompt Response: Respond to customer complaints and issues promptly. Acknowledge their concerns and assure them that their feedback is important. Aim to provide an initial response within 24-48 hours to demonstrate your commitment to addressing their concerns.

Active Listening: Practice active listening when communicating with customers. Allow them to fully express their concerns without interruption. Show empathy and understanding, and ask clarifying questions to gather all the necessary information to resolve the issue.

Empathetic and Professional Communication: Maintain a respectful and professional tone in all customer interactions. Empathize with their frustration or disappointment, and assure them that you are dedicated to resolving the problem. Avoid getting defensive or confrontational, even if the complaint seems unjustified.

Investigate the Issue: Gather all relevant information and investigate the issue thoroughly. Review the order details, product specifications, and any relevant communication records to understand the situation fully. If necessary, consult with your production or fulfillment partners to get a comprehensive understanding of the problem.

Take Ownership and Accountability: Take responsibility for the issue and assure the customer that you will work towards a resolution. Avoid passing blame or making excuses. Show that you value their satisfaction and are committed to finding a solution.

Offer Solutions: Provide practical and fair solutions to address the customer's concerns. Offer options such as replacement, refund, store credit, or free shipping for future orders, depending on the nature of the issue. Consider the customer's preferences and be flexible in finding a resolution that satisfies both parties.

Timely Resolution: Strive to resolve the complaint or issue as quickly as possible. Set realistic timelines for resolution and keep the customer informed of the progress. Communicate any delays or unexpected challenges transparently to manage their expectations.

Document and Learn: Keep records of customer complaints, the steps taken for resolution, and any outcomes. Use this information to identify recurring issues or patterns and implement measures to prevent similar problems in the future. Continuously learn from customer feedback to improve your products, processes, and customer service.

Learn from Negative Feedback: Use negative feedback as an opportunity to learn and grow. Analyze the root causes of the complaints and identify areas for improvement in your product quality, design accuracy, packaging, or customer support. Address these issues to prevent future occurrences.

Training and Support: Provide training and support to your customer service team to handle complaints effectively. Equip them with the knowledge and skills to address various scenarios, communicate clearly, and resolve issues in a satisfactory manner. Foster a customer-centric culture throughout your organization.

Review and Revise Policies: Regularly review your return, refund, and customer support policies to ensure they are fair, transparent, and aligned with industry standards. Make necessary revisions based on customer feedback and evolving needs.

Follow-Up: After resolving the complaint or issue, follow up with the customer to ensure their satisfaction and check if any further assistance is needed. This demonstrates your commitment to their happiness and helps build long-term customer relationships.

By effectively managing customer complaints and issues, you can turn a potentially negative experience into a positive one. Use these situations as opportunities to improve your products, services, and overall customer experience. A customer-centric approach will help build trust, loyalty, and a strong reputation for your print-on-demand business.

9.3 Frequently Asked Questions

1. What is print-on-demand (POD)?

    Print-on-demand is a business model where products, such as t-shirts, hoodies, or mugs, are produced and shipped to customers only after an order is placed. This eliminates the need for inventory management and allows for customization and personalization options.

2. How does print-on-demand work?

    In a print-on-demand business, you design or curate products, create digital files of your designs, and upload them to a POD platform. When a customer places an order, the platform prints the design on the chosen product and ships it directly to the customer on your behalf.

3. What products can I sell through print-on-demand?

Print-on-demand platforms offer a wide range of products, including t-shirts, tank tops,   hoodies, sweatshirts, hats, phone cases, tote bags, and more. The specific product options may vary depending on the POD platform you choose.

4. How do I get started with print-on-demand?

To start a print-on-demand business, you need to follow these steps:
1. Create or source your designs.
2. Choose a print-on-demand platform.
3. Set up an account and upload your designs.
4. Customize your product offerings, such as selecting colors and sizes.
5. Launch your online store and start promoting your products.

5. Do I need to have design skills to start a print-on-demand business?

While having design skills can be an advantage, you don't necessarily need them to start a print-on-demand business. Many platforms offer design templates that you can customize with text or simple modifications. You can also hire designers or use design services to create unique designs for your products.

6. How do I promote and market my print-on-demand products?

To promote your print-on-demand products, you can utilize various marketing strategies, including:
1. Building an online presence through a website or social media platforms.
2. Engaging with your target audience through content marketing, such as blog posts or videos.
3. Running targeted online advertisements.
4. Collaborating with influencers or affiliates to showcase your products.

5. Offering special promotions or discounts to attract customers.

7. Can I use copyrighted or trademarked designs on my print-on-demand products?

- No, you should not use copyrighted or trademarked designs without proper authorization. It is important to respect intellectual property rights and only use designs that you have the legal right to use. Create original designs or use licensed artwork to avoid legal issues.

8.How do I handle customer service for my print-on-demand business?

- Customer service is crucial for your print-on-demand business. You can handle customer inquiries, order issues, and general support through various channels, such as email, live chat, or social media messaging. Respond promptly, address concerns professionally, and provide assistance to ensure customer satisfaction.

9. How do I price my print-on-demand products?
- When pricing your products, consider factors such as production costs, platform fees, shipping expenses, and desired profit margins. Research market trends and competitor pricing to ensure your prices are competitive. Experiment with different pricing strategies and monitor customer response to optimize your pricing strategy.

10. How long does it take to fulfill an order in print-on-demand?

- The fulfillment time can vary depending on the print-on-demand platform and the complexity of the design. Typically, it takes a few days for production and processing before the product is shipped to the customer. Factors like order volume and shipping location can also impact the overall delivery time.

11.   Can I sell my print-on-demand products internationally?

·   Yes, many print-on-demand platforms offer international shipping options. This allows you to sell your products to customers worldwide. However, keep in mind that shipping times and costs may vary depending on the destination country.

Conclusion:

Congratulations! You have reached the end of "The Ultimate Guide to Print-on-Demand T-Shirts." By absorbing the valuable insights, strategies, and best practices shared in this ebook, you are now equipped to venture into the world of print-on-demand apparel, specifically focused on t-shirts. Remember, success in this field requires creativity, adaptability, and perseverance. Embrace the ever-evolving fashion landscape, experiment with unique designs, and enjoy the journey of building a thriving print-on-demand t-shirt business.